ROOK

GREAT SPOTTED
WOODPECKER

WOOD WARBLE

HONEYSUCKLE

FALLOW DEER

WOOD-PIGEON

WOOD WOUNDWORT

WOOD AVENS
HERB BENNET

WOOD ANEMONE

BLUE TIT

HERB ROBERT.

PRIMROSE

SILVER-WASHED
FRITILLARY

OAK
BUSH-CRICK

BLUEBELL

BANK VOLE

COMMON SHREW

CUCKOO PINT

Graham Underhill

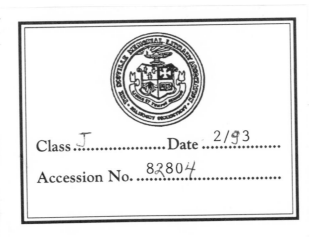
Oxford University Press   1983

Oxford University Press, Walton Street, Oxford OX2 6DP

Oxford London Glasgow
New York Toronto Melbourne Auckland
Kuala Lumpur Singapore Hong Kong Tokyo
Delhi Bombay Calcutta Madras Karachi
Nairobi Dar es Salaam Cape Town

and associated companies in
Beirut Berlin Ibadan Mexico City Nicosia

Oxford is a trade mark of Oxford University Press

ISBN 0 19 273153 X

The woodblock type on the cover
and title page is from the
collection in the Department of
Typography at Reading University.

Typeset by Keyspools Ltd, Golborne, Lancs
Printed in Hong Kong

OUT
OF THE
WOOD

To Emma

ONE autumn long ago a jay buried an acorn in a clearing in the forest. The jay was a wise bird, with a knowing bright eye like all his crow brothers, and he hid acorns when they were plentiful to keep him in food through the long hard winter. He was also, sometimes, a careless bird, forgetful of his acorns' hiding places, and so it was that this particular acorn remained uneaten.

When spring came and the bright sun began to warm the earth, the hidden acorn split open, pushed down a searching white root, and slowly unfurled its first leaves into the warm air.

England in those days, was a very different place from the country we know today. Forests covered most of the land and through these forests wandered red deer, wild boar and sometimes bears and wolves. Our forefathers made clearings in the forest where they could grow crops and let their animals browse, and it was on the edge of just such a clearing, not far from a tiny village, that the acorn began to grow.

The little oak seedling had a hard struggle to survive at first. The year's new explosion of greenery threatened to smother the young sapling, but the acorn had been hidden near a bramble bush, which soon threw its thorny stems over the new tree and protected it from the hungry forest animals.

In the mellow autumn air, twenty-five years later, a swineherd slept at the foot of a sturdy young oak tree. The tree had grown considerably and was even bearing its own crop of acorns. The pigs were rooting contentedly among the fallen leaves and grasses, when suddenly a stranger approached. He moved quietly, carrying a simple staff. He was clearly used to travelling through the wood. A dry branch snapped beneath the stranger's foot, and the swineherd woke with a start.

'Don't be afraid,' said the stranger, 'I come in peace.'

'Yes, yes I think you do,' replied the swineherd with relief. He had heard many terrifying tales of raiders who came from the sea, to burn, kill and steal. You could never be too careful.

'It's a sad state of affairs, when you can't take a nap in the woods without being scared half to death by a piece of old wood!' laughed the stranger. 'It's the Danes that you fear, I suppose? . . . One day, I hope we shall all live in peace together.'

The swineherd was astonished. 'Live in peace with them! Those barbarians?' The stranger grew more serious.

'Remember that we Saxons once behaved in much the same way, when we first came to this country, destroying what we could not understand. But now we have learnt to live peacefully, using our time and efforts to provide food and shelter. Our children grow up without fear or hunger. Instead, there is knowledge and friendship.' The swineherd scratched his head as the stranger continued.

'Consider the woodland around us. When your village was first built, your forefathers used to cut timber anywhere they chose; their animals could wander where they pleased eating all the young shoots and seedlings. People soon realised that the forest was being destroyed, and it was being destroyed because there was no understanding, no control, no co-operation. Now, the forest has a woodward, who decides when and where trees may be cut, and where the animals may graze, so that parts of the wood are allowed time to recover. If there was more understanding and co-operation like that between Saxon and Dane, then our differences might be reconciled, and we might be able to recover like the trees. Who knows, one day a single king may rule over us all.'

'But these Danes are not even Christians,' objected the swineherd.

'Some of the Danish leaders have been converted,' continued the stranger, 'and some of our own womenfolk still wear pouches of polished stones and charms, even though they believe in the one God. You see how two beliefs may sit peacefully side by side. Anyway, that's enough of my preaching. I must be on my way.'

'My head is buzzing with all your wisdom,' said the swineherd. 'Please, tell me your name before you go!'

'My name is Alfred of Wessex,' shouted the stranger as he strode off between the trees.

As the years passed by, events turned out much as Alfred had hoped. His wise thoughts and just actions became the basis of English Law. The Danes that settled in England built their own villages, and many became Christians. Gradually the Saxons and Danes intermarried and a single king did rule over the English people. But there is never an end to conflict and soon fresh bands of raiders came, beaching their fearsome longships on the shores and riverbanks in search of new homelands.

All this while the oak tree grew on. It had been pollarded several times: its upper branches removed to supply wood for house building, tool making and furniture. The Saxons were wise users of timber and rarely destroyed a whole tree when carefully chosen branches would suffice for the job in hand.

The villagers also farmed two open fields in which each family had its share of narrow strips. The day came when it was decided to make a third field by clearing some of the more open scrub-land on the margin of the wood. There were only a few large trees here, because most of the older ones had died or been used in the building of the village church.

Clearing land was always a laborious process with only hand tools and oxen to help in the task. First, the grass and bushes had to be set on fire, and then the hard work of clearing could really begin. On this occasion the burning was going well when a sudden gust of wind caught the flames and swept them rapidly towards the dense woodland where the oak tree stood. All could have been lost, but the same wind that had spread the fire also brought great clouds and torrential rain. The rain quenched the flames that leapt and licked about the tree, but not before the searing heat had scorched the bark black.

THE tree grew steadily towards maturity, and life in the woods and fields continued almost unchanged. But then, quite unexpectedly, events in the village took a different turn. William of Normandy had conquered England in 1066. He began at once to make changes to the country, one of which was a new overlord for the villagers, a Norman knight, whose castle had been built just a few miles away. It was to this Norman knight that the villagers now owed their service and paid their taxes. The village and all the land for miles around was soon declared a Royal Hunting Forest, and a special court was set up to enforce new forest laws. These laws forbade the cutting of trees and the killing of deer and wild boar and, worst of all, the villagers were forbidden to hedge their fields to prevent all the wild animals from destroying their crops. As you can imagine, no one was too pleased with the new overlord, but relief was at hand.

Amongst the inhabitants of the village there was an archer, as fine a man as ever bent a bow in England. Despite his lowly origins, he soon earned the respect of his Norman master by winning many prizes for him in tournaments. 'An archer is known by his aim not by his arrows,' was how his lordship chose to put it.

After one particularly successful contest for the archer, his Norman master was moved to offer him some sort of reward. Without pausing for a moment's thought the archer replied 'I would like you to give to the people of my village the right to use their lands in the old way. And the extent of the land to be fixed shall be the area that I can encompass by shooting a quiverful of arrows.'

The Norman lord was astonished by such a request, but knew that he had to agree. The archer went to prepare for the attempt, knowing that if his last arrow did not land on the exact spot where he started, he would forfeit his prize. There was no room for mistakes. He selected the finest stave of yew he could find to make a new longbow, and five straight ash sticks for his arrow shafts. He would use the pinion feathers from a grey goose for the flights. From these materials he fashioned a bow and arrows of near perfection. No man had ever made finer.

His bowmanship, on the calm winter morning chosen for the event, was no less masterful. The Norman lord was so impressed by the archer's skills that as well as returning their lands to them he gave the village people freemen rights to enough timber each year for house building and fencing, and the right to gather all the firewood they could knock down from the trees by weeding hook or shepherd's crook.

One of the arrows fired by the archer had embedded itself in the trunk of the oak tree. The tree became a boundary marker, and as a result was spared further pollarding. During the next hundred years, the oak was left alone, and allowed to renew and spread its massive branches.

In its favoured position on the edge of the open fields the tree grew through its middle age. Its huge crown of branches grew free from the competition of other trees, and the nearby woodland provided shelter against the force of the prevailing winds. Many forms of wildlife made their home in the oak, from tiny wasp larvae to the majestic tawny owl who slept all day, hidden among the leaves.

For many generations the lives of the villagers remained hard. They lived on from season to season, ruled by the descendants of that first Norman lord who had been forced to return their rights to the land. Year after year the harvest was brought in, until one terrible autumn when the fields remained still and silent. The crops were left untouched for the wild birds and harvest mice to feed upon, only finally to be laid low by the harsh winds and frosts. All winter through, no smoke rose from the dwellings in the village, and even when spring came no one stirred on the land. The Black Death was raging in Britain. The few survivors in the village had abandoned their homes, desperate to escape the disease.

In the years that followed, nature began to reclaim the village. The straw and turf roofs of cottages, supported only by frail sticks, collapsed. The mud walls, left unprotected, were washed away by the rain. Luxuriant growths of nettles, brambles, grasses and wild flowers grew unchecked over the remaining signs of human habitation. The woodland, left to itself, grew dense, whilst the fields became a wasteland of scrub, dotted with thickets of ash, hazel, birch and elder. Given time all would have become a forest, such as there had been before men walked this land, but then a new sound was heard, a sound that heralded further changes in the lands around the oak tree.

THE sound was the bleating of sheep. Hundreds and hundreds of sheep, whose ever nibbling teeth began to check the advance of nature and turn into pasture the land that had once been field. Because of the Black Death, there were too few people to work the strips in the old way, so it was thought best to use the land for grazing sheep. Sheep almost looked after themselves, and they provided a good return of wool for only a little effort.

One fine spring day a shepherd was tending his woolly flock. He was leaning against the now massive trunk of the oak tree, on the sheltered side, with his sheep in view all around him. Each sheep had a raddle mark on its back so that it could be distinguished from all the others when its owner claimed it at shearing time. The shepherd's life could be lonely and hard, but at least he was paid, unlike his ancestors, and could in many ways think himself a much happier man.

From his vantage point the shepherd was able to watch the hurdle maker at work among the stumps of the hazel coppice. Some of the wood had been set aside to make the hurdles which were needed in great numbers to pen and control the sheep. One seventh part of the coppice was cut down each year in the early spring and not touched again until its turn came round again seven years later. By this time many new stems would have grown from the old roots. After felling, the hazel stems were sorted according to size. The hurdle maker then arranged his simple tools and began work. First he arranged the upright poles in the mould, which was a curved log with ten holes bored in it. Then he split some hazel rods into thin strips with a billhook and wove them in and out of the uprights to form the finished hurdle.

There was something soothing and almost hypnotic in the sight of the hurdle maker practising his craft. To the shepherd, as he watched, all seemed timeless and unchanging; he dozed quietly in the spring sunshine and his sheep grazed on contentedly.

IT is often true that when all is apparently calm, great changes are at work on the land. Many men were riding to prosperity on the backs of the humble wool-giving sheep. A new village began to thrive near the oak tree, surrounded by enclosed sheep pastures, and founded by farmers made rich by the wool trade. The new cottages provided homes for labourers on the farms, and also for the spinners, dyers and weavers who worked in backrooms and outhouses, converting the wool into cloth. The cottages were not like the frail huts of the old village, but were now built soundly using frameworks of oak.

The house builders would search the woods for oaks with suitable curved boughs or trunks. These would form the main supporting frames of a cottage. The builders rejected the boughs of the ageing oak which stood in a green clearing near the village. Its trunk had become hollow, and the massive branches were too twisted for building straight houses. They would have been of more use to a ship-wright looking for 'knees' and 'elbows' – the sturdy bent timbers required for a ship's framework.

Once cut, the curved boughs would be brought to the building site and split along their lengths to provide pairs of curved timbers that were the 'splitting image' of one another. The pairs, jointed together, would be raised to form the main 'A' shaped structure of the cottage, to which the framework of roof and walls could then be fixed with oak pegs. The spaces left in the framework of the walls were then filled with wattle, which was made using hazel rods and stakes of oak, daubed or plastered over to keep out the weather. Finally, the roof was covered with a straw thatch and tied down with hazel rods.

Not only were the houses made mostly of wood, but the villagers also warmed themselves and cooked their food on wood fires, carried their goods in wooden carts, sat on wooden chairs, ate from wooden plates on wooden tables, and at night, put up wooden shutters and slept on wooden beds.

A pedlar, who regularly travelled the rutted tracks from village to village, selling knives, needles, pots and fine thread, paused one day to rest in the shade of the aged oak. A thin wisp of smoke, rising from the woods, showed him that the charcoal burners were at work. These men and their families moved about the country living in simple huts near to their charcoal hearths. The pedlar knew that they were often also very good customers. Setting off into the woods, he soon found their camp, and passed the next few hours in pleasant talk and trade among his smoky friends. They offered him food, and as he ate he watched the charcoal burners build a hearth out of a pile of logs that had been dragged to the camp. They told him how later it would be covered in straw and earth, lit in the central hollow, and then sealed to block out the air. During the firing it was necessary to watch all night and all day in case the fire should fan and break out, blazing the wood to useless ashes. In the right conditions, the wood turned slowly into the glossy black charcoal that was so much in demand for the metal smelting furnaces, glassworks and forges.

Unlike the villagers who lived all their lives in one place, travelling folk like the charcoal burners and the pedlar, were daily aware of the dwindling number of trees, and the gradual retreat of the woods. The activities of most working people of Britain depended upon the supply of wood, and as the country prospered, so the demand for wood grew. Not only charcoal burners, but builders, carpenters, ship-wrights and miners were using timber in such quantities that the natural regeneration of the woodlands could not keep pace. To make matters worse, many woods were being turned into farmlands. It was not surprising therefore, that the timber shortage became a serious problem in the seventeenth century. Not until after the Civil War, when Charles II had regained his throne, did landowners begin to plant trees to try to meet future demands for timber.

THE village continued to prosper, unchanged for the most part, well into the next century. The tree had become part of the everyday scenery of the village, the focal point of fairs and celebrations, and a much used meeting place. Travellers, too poor to stay at the village inn, would shelter for the night in its hollow trunk. In hot weather the visiting magistrates and tax collectors would conduct their business in the shade of its spreading boughs. Many fiery sermons were delivered by wandering preachers as they stood on rickety pulpits amongst the roots.

As time passed, one local landowning family, the Oakfields, became wealthier and wealthier. They farmed the land, embarked on foreign trading ventures, and made alliances with other wealthy families. Eventually Lord Oakfield, as he was now called, bought out the remaining yeoman farmers in the district, and made himself landlord of the entire village and its surroundings.

In the seventeen-sixties a fine new house was built for Lord Oakfield, in the latest continental fashion. The proud Lord had recently discovered 'landscape' through reading travel books and looking at paintings, and as he gazed from his new windows he found the view sadly lacking in picturesqueness. In a trice a landscape gardener was employed and ordered to create a fine 'natural' park which would set off the charms of the house. When the plans had been carefully drawn up and the land measured out with transit and level, the landscape gardener gathered together his workforce and began to turn his plans into a splendid reality. A lake was created by the damming of a stream, avenues and drives were made, hundreds of saplings were planted, larger trees were uprooted and repositioned (as though they were no more than chess pieces), and an obelisk and 'ruin' were built to add detail and interest to the design. Unfortunately the village had to go. A collection of timber and straw houses would simply have ruined the view. It was completely demolished and reconstructed on a new site well hidden from the fine house.

Luckily the ancient oak had a wild and rugged quality that appealed to the landscape gardener, so it was left untouched as a feature of the finished landscape. It was also fitted with a large iron chain to help some of its vast limbs in their struggle against gravity.

When the fortunes of a large country estate are in the hands of one family, all is well if the head of that family is wise in the running of the estate, thoughtful and just in dealing with tenants and employees, and careful in the management of money. Such was the case with the Oakfield family, and for many years the estate prospered. Even the villagers grew content, once the memory of the moving of their dwellings had begun to fade. The park and all that it contained slowly matured, and the great oak grew more and more gnarled.

In time, the third Lord Oakfield inherited the house, the estate and the oak. He had been an irresponsible boy, and a constant source of worry to his parents. When sent to a foreign university, in an attempt to induce in him a more cultured attitude to life, the young man succeeded only in developing a spendthrift nature and a liking for bad company. Now that he had come into his inheritance, he was able to indulge to the full his new found tastes for gambling, drinking and high living.

It was not at all long before the third Lord Oakfield ran up huge debts. To appease his creditors he sold the tenanted farms and the home farm to boot. He sold timber from the fine avenues in the park, but still could not raise sufficient funds. He reduced the number of servants, sold horses and carriages, and eventually one third of the park itself. Even the lead from the roof was hauled away.

In spite of all this, Lord Oakfield continued his debauched way of life, and one summer evening, during a drunken party with his friends, the house was accidentally set on fire. The few remaining servants fought the blaze gallantly, but they were unable to prevent the fire from destroying both the house and the wretched young man's fortunes.

That autumn, in keeping with the desolation of the scene, a terrible storm descended on the park. Hail, thunder, lightning, and raging winds ripped and whipped through the branches of the oak as it shook its bronzed leaves. The rotting trunk was no longer able to stand such an onslaught; it split from top to bottom sending its massive boughs crashing to the ground on either side.

THE venerable old tree was mortally wounded, and the following spring was the last time that any fresh leaves appeared on its battered branches. As spring turned into summer, the oak's remaining grandeur collapsed beneath its weight of years and leaves.

The oak, which seemed as much part of the landscape as the earth from which it had sprung, was dead at last. It had survived the rigours of a thousand winters, and seen many changes of face and fortune. It had supplied wood for our ancestors in its early days. It had produced countless millions of leaves, which meant life not only for the tree itself but also for millions of insects and their larvae. Its acorns had fed swine, squirrels, birds and mice, every autumn for ten centuries. Its branches and bark, and later its hollow trunk, had been home to everything from bats to beetles, and from birds to beggars. Lichens, mosses and ferns had grown on the tree, and even in death, its decaying roots provided nourishment for swelling fungi and wood-boring insects. A full and fascinating life for just one tree, and the story was not quite over yet.

One early summer's day, a heavy waggon made its way across the grass towards the fallen tree. The three men bobbed and swayed as they rode, clutching an assortment of saws and axes. The carter perched on the shafts, guiding the horses over the uneven ground. They had been sent by a farmer, to remove all remainders of the tree, which lay now in what had become a meadow. Two days of sawing and chopping later, the job was done. By then the men had delivered five waggon loads of logs to crackle on festive fires.

The village carpenter also managed to salvage a considerable amount of sound timber from the larger boughs, and he stored this away to season in his timber shed. He was a man skilled in joinery, wood-turning and carving, with an artist's sensitivity to the qualities of his material. It was inevitable, therefore, that when he used the seasoned timber to make first a table, then chairs and a carved chest for his home, the furniture should seem to contain something of the ancient spirit of the living tree.

LIKE all objects that are skilfully and honestly made from natural materials, the carpenter's oak furniture filled his house with a comforting presence. They were cherished by his family, and handed down from one generation to the next. And so it was that on a cold winter's evening, the children (in the picture) were gathered round that very same table, made from the wood of the oak that lived for a thousand years. They sorted and arranged their collection: an acorn, its cup like a fairy pipe; an oak apple; fantastically coloured and twisted leaves collected on a walk through the wood; a moth, dead but perfect; snail shells spiralling to nothing; a fragment from a blackbird's egg, blue and speckled brown. All this and more they lay out on the table, like treasure to wonder at.

Outside the warm cottage, beneath the frost-brightened stars, an acorn lay in a pot of soil, sown there by the three children. Come the spring, who knows what wonders may begin?

So the story is ended, and now if you wish, you may take a nature trail through the pages of this book. There is a chart to help you find all the wild plants and creatures on the list; but as on all nature trails you must use your eyes very carefully, and not make too much noise.

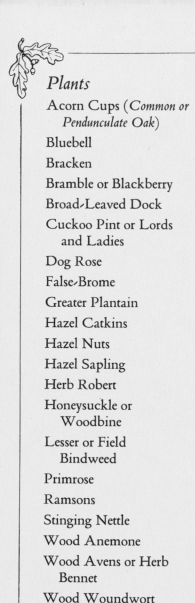

Plants

- Acorn Cups (*Common or Pendunculate Oak*)
- Bluebell
- Bracken
- Bramble or Blackberry
- Broad-Leaved Dock
- Cuckoo Pint or Lords and Ladies
- Dog Rose
- False-Brome
- Greater Plantain
- Hazel Catkins
- Hazel Nuts
- Hazel Sapling
- Herb Robert
- Honeysuckle or Woodbine
- Lesser or Field Bindweed
- Primrose
- Ramsons
- Stinging Nettle
- Wood Anemone
- Wood Avens or Herb Bennet
- Wood Woundwort

Birds

- Barn Owl
- Blue Tit
- Chaffinch
- Great Tit
- Great Spotted Woodpecker
- Green Woodpecker
- Jay
- Long-Tailed Tit
- Nuthatch
- Rook
- Swallow
- Tawny Owl
- Tree Creeper
- Woodcock
- Wood-Pigeon
- Wood Warbler

Fungi

- Death Cap
- Glistening Ink Cap
- Golden Ear
- Oyster Cap

Insects

- Cardinal Beetle
- Cockchafer
- Copper Underwing Moth
- Gatekeeper or Hedge Brown Butterfly
- Oak Bush-Cricket
- Mottled Umber Moth
- Peppered Moth
- Purple Hairstreak Butterfly
- Silver-Washed Fritillary Butterfly
- Small Tortoiseshell Butterfly
- Stag Beetle
- Tanner Beetle

Galls

(eggs and larvae of tiny wasps inhabit these)

- Cherry Galls
- Oak Apple Gall
- Oak Marble Gall
- Oak Spangle Gall

Mammals

- Bank Vole
- Brown Hare
- Common Shrew
- Fallow Deer
- Greater Horseshoe Bat
- Hedgehog
- Natterer's Bat
- Pipistrelle Bat
- Red Deer
- Red Fox
- Red Squirrel
- Wood Mouse or Long Tailed Fieldmouse

Snails

- Common or Garden Snail
- White-Lipped Banded Snail

Larvae

- Bramble Leaf Miner (*larva of moth Nepticula Aurella*)
- 'Looper' Caterpillar of Peppered Moth
- White Admiral Caterpillar

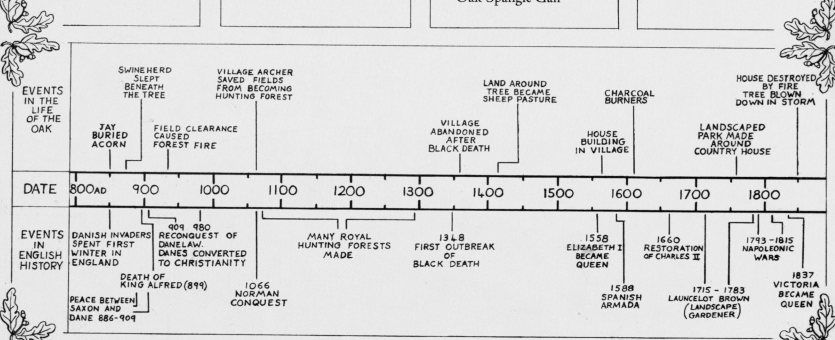

EVENTS IN THE LIFE OF THE OAK

SWINEHERD SLEPT BENEATH THE TREE	VILLAGE ARCHER SAVED FIELDS FROM BECOMING HUNTING FOREST	LAND AROUND TREE BECAME SHEEP PASTURE	HOUSE DESTROYED BY FIRE TREE BLOWN DOWN IN STORM
JAY BURIED ACORN	FIELD CLEARANCE CAUSED FOREST FIRE	VILLAGE ABANDONED AFTER BLACK DEATH	CHARCOAL BURNERS
		HOUSE BUILDING IN VILLAGE	LANDSCAPED PARK MADE AROUND COUNTRY HOUSE

DATE 800 AD 900 1000 1100 1200 1300 1400 1500 1600 1700 1800

EVENTS IN ENGLISH HISTORY

DANISH INVADERS SPENT FIRST WINTER IN ENGLAND

909 RECONQUEST OF DANELAW. DANES CONVERTED TO CHRISTIANITY

980

MANY ROYAL HUNTING FORESTS MADE

1348 FIRST OUTBREAK OF BLACK DEATH

1558 ELIZABETH I BECAME QUEEN

1660 RESTORATION OF CHARLES II

1793 - 1815 NAPOLEONIC WARS

DEATH OF KING ALFRED (899)

1066 NORMAN CONQUEST

1588 SPANISH ARMADA

1715 - 1783 LAUNCELOT BROWN (LANDSCAPE GARDENER)

1837 VICTORIA BECAME QUEEN

PEACE BETWEEN SAXON AND DANE 886-909